DR. BOB'S
AMAZING WORLD OF
ANIMALS
MOOSE

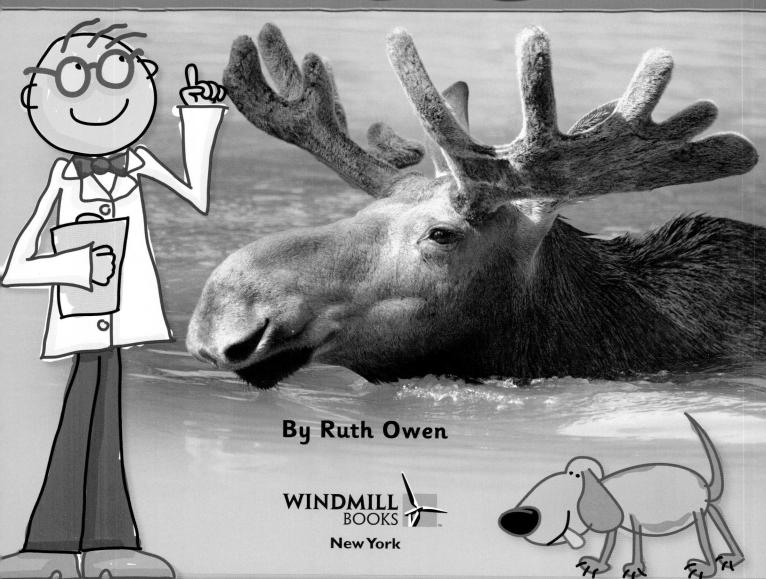

By Ruth Owen

WINDMILL BOOKS

New York

Published in 2014 by Windmill Books, An Imprint of Rosen Publishing
29 East 21st Street, New York, NY 10010

Editor for Ruby Tuesday Books Ltd: Mark J. Sachner
US Editor: Joshua Shadowens
Designer: Trudi Webb

Photo credits: Cover, 1, 4–5, 7, 8–9, 10–11, 12–13, 14–15, 16–17, 22–23, 24–25, 26–27, 28–29, 30
© Shutterstock; 13 (top), 20 © Wikipedia Creative Commons; 18 © Hagerty Ryan, U.S. Fish and
Wildlife Service; 19, 21 © FLPA.

Library of Congress Cataloging-in-Publication Data

Owen, Ruth 1967-
 Moose / by Ruth Owen.
     pages cm. — (Dr. Bob's amazing world of animals)
Includes index.
ISBN 978-1-47779-036-6 (library) — ISBN 978-1-47779-037-3 (pbk.) —
ISBN 978-1-47779-038-0 (6-pack)
1. Moose—Juvenile literature. I. Title.
QL737.U55.O936 2014
599.65'7—dc23

                                  2013026843

Manufactured in the United States of America

CPSIA Compliance Information: Batch #BW14WM: For Further Information contact Windmill Books, New York, New York at 1-866-478-0556

Contents

The Moose

Welcome to my amazing world of animals. Today, we are visiting forests in North America to find out about moose.

A female, or cow, moose

Let's investigate...

Hank's **WOOF OF WISDOM!**

Moose are a type of deer. They are the largest members of the deer family.

A male moose is called a bull. A female moose is called a cow. Baby moose are called calves.

A male, or bull, moose

Moose is the name used for these large deer in North America. In Europe, they are known as elk.

The Land of the Moose

Moose live in northern parts of North America, Europe, and Asia.

Moose live in places that are cool for large parts of the year and often very cold in winter.

North America

Europe

Asia

Africa

Pacific Ocean

South America

Atlantic Ocean

Indian Ocean

Australia

Antarctica

The areas marked in red on the map are where moose can be found.

Moose live in evergreen forests and among trees that lose their leaves in winter.

These animals spend some of their time in water. So they make their homes in places where there are lakes, streams, and swamps called **muskegs**.

Moose Bodies

Moose have long faces, large, heavy bodies, and thin, stilt-like legs. Their hair can be golden-brown, reddish-brown, dark brown, or blackish-brown.

Dewlap, or bell

A moose has a flap of hairy skin hanging from its throat. Some people call this a dewlap, while others call it a bell.

A moose's long legs are perfect for stepping over fallen trees in forests. They also help the moose wade through water and swamps, and plow through thick snow.

Moose Size Chart

Bull Moose

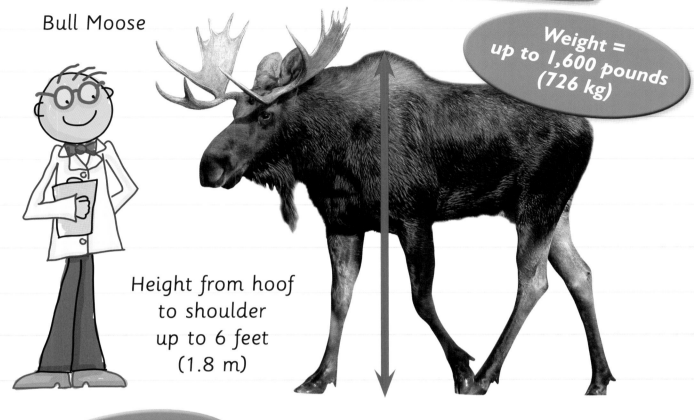

Weight =
up to 1,600 pounds
(726 kg)

Height from hoof
to shoulder
up to 6 feet
(1.8 m)

Weight =
up to 900 pounds
(408 kg)

Cow Moose

Height from hoof
to shoulder
up to 6 feet
(1.8 m)

Awesome Antlers

Adult male moose have huge, branch-like antlers. Their antlers can grow as long as 6 feet (1.8 m) from tip to tip.

Each year, in the early winter, a male moose's antlers fall off. Then, when spring arrives, they begin to regrow.

New antlers growing

Velvet-like material

At first, the new antlers are soft and spongy. They are covered with a velvet-like material.

By late summer, a male's antlers are fully grown. Now, they are hard and bony.

Fully-grown antlers

The velvet-like covering gets dry, and the male moose rubs off the covering against trees.

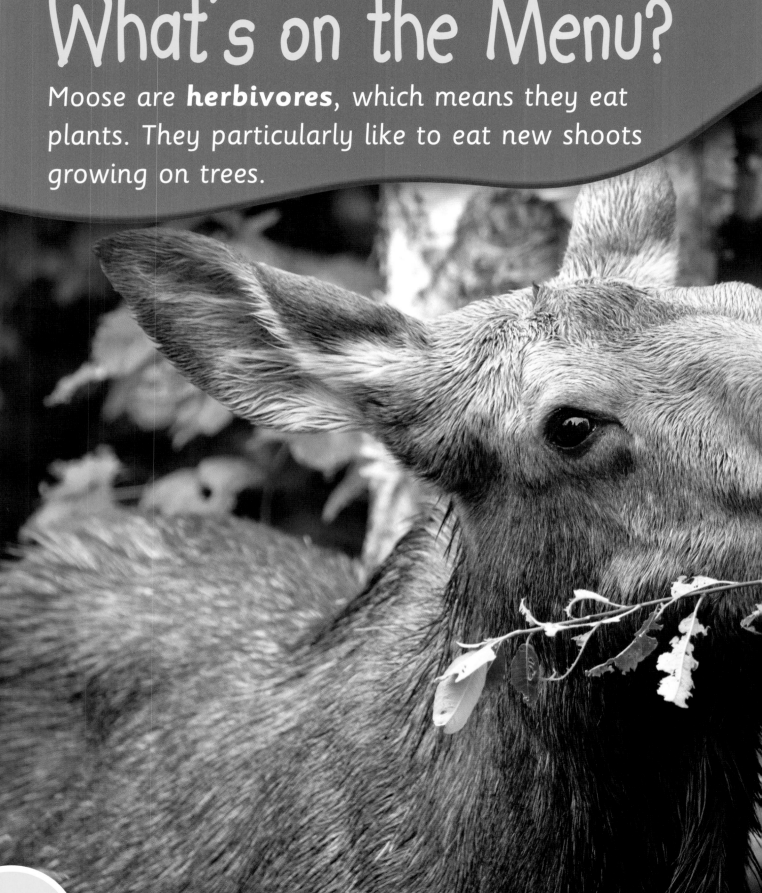

What's on the Menu?

Moose are **herbivores**, which means they eat plants. They particularly like to eat new shoots growing on trees.

A moose has eaten the bark on this tree trunk.

For these very tall plant-eaters, it's easier to eat bushes and trees than low-growing plants. So moose often feed on twigs, leaves, and bark from tree trunks.

A moose's favorite trees to eat include willow, aspen, and balsam firs.

Hank's
WOOF OF WISDOM!

In the language of the native American Algonquins, the word "moose" means "eater of twigs."

Water Moose

A moose can often be seen **foraging** for **aquatic** plants that grow in lakes, swamps, and streams.

A moose will wade out into a lake to find a juicy meal. It might even dive underwater to munch on a plant that's growing at the bottom of a lake!

A moose foraging

14

Moose are strong swimmers, and will swim at up to 6 miles per hour (10 km/h).

A moose swimming

Because their large, hairy bodies are suited for cold weather, moose can get too hot when temperatures warm up. So swimming in a cool lake is an excellent way to cool off!

Ready for Winter

When the icy-cold, northern winters come around, moose are all set for survival.

Every hair in a moose's thick coat is hollow, like a straw. Air gets trapped inside the hollow hairs and creates a layer of warming **insulation** around the animal.

When all the green leaves and shoots are gone, moose will eat **shrubs**, twigs, and pine cones.

If there is **moss** growing under the snow, a moose can use its large hooves to scrape away the snow and reveal this tasty food.

Getting the Girls

All summer, a male moose is growing antlers. Finally, in the fall, he is looking his best for the **mating season**.

Hank's
WOOF OF WISDOM!

In the world of the moose, the bigger your antlers are, the more handsome you are!

During September and October, males make loud, bellowing noises to attract females.

Often two males will fight over a female. The two fighters go head to head with their antlers locked together.

The males push each other and battle with their antlers until one fighter gives in. The winner gets the girl!

Mini Moose

In May or June, about eight months after mating, a female moose gives birth.

A moose usually gives birth to one or two calves at the same time.

Mother moose

Calves drinking milk

A newborn calf has a reddish-brown coat. The little moose weighs about 30 pounds (14 kg).

Within a few hours of being born, moose calves start drinking milk from their mothers.

Female moose feed their calves while standing up and while sitting down!

Growing Fast

At just one week old, a moose calf can swim well and run faster than a human.

By two weeks old, the calf is eating plants. It still drinks milk from its mother, though.

The combination of milk and plant food helps the calf grow fast.

By the time a calf is five to six months old, it can weigh as much as 500 pounds (227 kg)!

A Calf's First Year

A moose calf gains weight and grows bigger, fast. By the fall, the calf stops drinking milk and eats only plants.

A calf lives with its mother until it is about one year old.

When its mother gives birth to a new calf in the spring, she chases the one-year-old calf away. Now the young moose must live alone and begin its grown-up life.

A young male moose will begin growing small, lumpy antlers in his first year.

Antler

A young female moose is ready to have a calf of her own when she is just over two years old.

Moose Enemies

Moose may be very large animals, but they are still in danger from big, powerful meat-eaters that share their **habitat**.

Black bears, brown bears, and packs of wolves will all attack and kill a moose.

If an adult moose is attacked, it will kick its enemy. Males use their antlers to defend themselves, too.

Black bear

Brown bear

Wolf pack

Calves are especially in danger from large **predators**.

Watching for danger

A mother moose will bravely defend her calf if an enemy attacks. She runs at the predator and kicks at it with her large hooves.

Don't Make a Moose Mad

Moose are gentle plant-eaters, but if they feel threatened, they might charge at a person.

A scared or angry moose will put its ears flat. The hair on its back will rise up, too.

If you accidentally startle or upset a moose, very slowly walk away. If it runs toward you, hide behind something solid like a tree or car.

Never go near a female moose with a calf because she will think you want to hurt her baby.

People who visit places where moose live should never approach the animals. Enjoy watching these beautiful wild animals from a distance!

Glossary

aquatic (uh-KWAH-tik) Growing or living in water.

foraging (FOR-uj-ing) Searching for food.

habitat (HA-buh-tat) The place where an animal or plant normally lives. A habitat may be a forest, the ocean, or a backyard.

herbivores (UR-buh-vorz) Animals that only eat plants.

insulation (in-suh-LAY-shun) A substance or material that keeps something warm.

mating season (MAYT-ing SEE-zun) A time of year when the males and females of a particular type of animal get together to mate and produce young.

moss (MOS) A small, low-growing plant that usually grows in cool, damp places such as forests. Lots of moss plants will grow close together and look like a green carpet.

muskegs (MUS-kegz) Boggy, wet habitats where the ground is made up of layers of decaying, or rotting, plants, especially sphagnum moss.

predators (PREH-duh-terz) Animals that hunt and kill other animals for food.

shrubs (SHRUBZ) Woody plants with branches that are smaller than trees.

Dr. Bob's Fast Fact Board

A moose does not have very good eyesight. Its hearing and sense of smell are very good, though.

Over a short distance, a moose can run at up to 35 miles per hour (56 km/h).

During its first month, a moose calf's diet of milk and plants helps it gain one pound (0.5 kg) of weight each day!

Moose live for between 10 and 20 years.

Websites

For web resources related to the subject of this book, go to: **www.windmillbooks.com/weblinks** and select this book's title.

Read More

Arnold, Caroline. *A Moose's World*. Caroline Arnold's Animals. Mankato, MN: Picture Window Books, 2010.

Macken, JoAnn Early. *Moose*. Animals That Live in the Forest. New York: Gareth Stevens Leveled Readers, 2009.

Magby, Meryl. *Moose*. American Animals. New York: PowerKids Press, 2012.

Index